Piano Chords Three
(Numbers)

How to Play Songs By Ear Without Sheet Music
Using The Nashville Number System

MICAH BROOKS

PUBLISHING | EST. 1985

Also By Micah Brooks

The Piano Authority Series:

Piano Chords One (All Seven Natural Keys):
A Beginner's Guide To Simple Music Theory
and Playing Chords To Any Song Quickly

Piano Chords Two (All Flat and Sharp Keys):
A Beginner's Guide To Simple Music Theory
and Playing Chords To Any Song Quickly

The Guitar Authority Series:

Worship Guitar In Six Weeks:
A Complete Beginner's Guide to Learning
Rhythm Guitar for Christian Worship Music

42 Guitar Chords Everyone Should Know:
A Complete Step-By-Step Guide To Mastering
42 Of The Most Important Guitar Chords

Fast Guitar Chord Transitions:
A Beginner's Guide to Moving Quickly
Between Guitar Chords Like a Professional

Guitar Secrets Revealed:
Unconventional and Amazing Guitar Chords,
Professional Techniques, Capo Tricks,
Alternate Tunings, Head Math, Rhythm & More

Guitar Chord Flipbook: An Essential Acoustic and
Electric Guitar Chord Reference Manual
that Fits in your Guitar Case

Ukulele Authority Series:

Ukulele In Six Weeks:
How to Play Ukulele Chords Quickly
and Easily for Beginners, Kids, and Early Learners

Songbooks and Music:

Micah Brooks All Things New EP Songbook

Micah Brooks All Things New EP

Christian Books:

Forsaking All Others:
The book we wish we'd had when dating, engaged,
and in the early years of our marriage to set us up for future success.

21 Day Character Challenge:
A Daily Devotional and Bible Reading Plan

Galatians: A Fresh, New Six Day
Bible Study and Commentary

Ephesians: A Fresh, New Six Day
Bible Study and Commentary

James: A Fresh, New Five Day
Bible Study and Commentary

Copyright Information

Published by WorshipHeart Publishing

Cover Design by Micah Brooks Kennedy

Dedication

This book is dedicated to my friend, Jamie Harvill. I remember being an early twenty-something and having raw musical talent. I lacked so much by the way of skill. Jamie came alongside and taught me to hear harmony overtop vocal melody. We discussed the layering of audio in recording while keeping the less-is-more technique in the forefront. He explained to me how to hear chords as numbers being able to play any song in any key. Without you, Jamie, this book would not exist. Most of what I do musically would be far more limited. I have sincere admiration for you and am grateful for your involvement in my life.

Contents

Micah Brooks

Welcome: Why Numbers and What Are They?

Welcome!

Welcome to *Piano Chords Three: Numbers*! I am excited that you've decided to learn to play by ear. With this book, you'll have the training you need to do just that. As you work through this material, remind yourself often that being able to listen to a song and figure out the chords by ear is a learned skill. It's a process and the process will take time. You'll develop your new skill each time you practice like a great muscle that you are developing when you lift weights. The most important thing is that you can certainly do this!

How each chapter is structured

Each chapter is dedicated to a single number or set of numbers. This book is intentionally laid out so that you could reference a certain chord you need at a later date. You may also jump around in the book if you'd like as well. Most chapters can stand alone and do not need the previous material to be effective.

Music is math

You may be surprised to find out that there are only four chords that make up most pop songs. In fact, one of those four chords is actually just the fundamental chord, but with a shifted down bass note and sounds darker. This means that you only need to learn–and you absolutely can learn–how to hear, or be able to recognize, three main chords.

You'll need to know a little about music theory. I aim to give you the most practical and applicable section of music theory that you will ever need. There's no mention of accidentals or words like harmonic progression. Rather, I'll give you music theory concepts you can use every time you play. I employ this each moment I play my instruments and so can you. Trust me, you'll understand this material!

One more disclaimer, the method I propose next is basic. If you have music theory friends, they may either say "duh" or attempt to clutter this with more information. These are the basic building blocks for the theory that all musicians need. This is not a comprehensive study. To do that, go to Belmont University in Nashville, TN where I went, or to another music school. They know it all there. This is for those of us in the trenches. This is for anyone who wants the basics so that you can get out there and perform.

The Chords Scale (1, 2m, ⅓, 4, 5, 6m, ⅝, 1)

Music is built on notes which our ears perceive as tones. Notes join in series to create scales. The fundamental or root note of the scale is the tonic note. A chord is the addition of two or more notes played at the same time. Playing in a certain key means that you are playing music by the rules of particularly predefined tones that work well together. This working together is called being relative to one another. Every key has a fundamental or root chord. This is known as the 1 chord and will be the heart and soul of the first chapter.

Most beginner pianists learn to play scales. A musical scale is any set of musical notes ordered by fundamental frequency or pitch. Scales help to know in which key you are playing. A key is defined by how many sharp or flat notes it has. Flats and sharps are the black keys on the piano. For instance, the key of C uses only natural notes, or the white keys. If you flatten the B note–now the B becomes B♭–you have moved from the key of C into the key of F.

For our purposes in this book, we will use the key of C as our reference key. It serves us best because it only uses natural notes–again, no black key flat or sharp notes. Therefore, in the key of C, its major scale are these notes in ascending order: C, D, E, F, G, A, B, and then back to C.

Single note scales are helpful when determining the key of a song. On the other hand, a chord scale helps to know which notes build each of the main chords within the key. A three-note chord whose pitches can be arranged in perfect thirds from one another is called a triad. Like the major scale using single notes has an ascending sound, going up the chords scale also has upward motion.

The basis for this book is that you'll understand each of the numbers along the chords scale and be able to recognize them by ear. The numbers are:

$$1, 2m, \frac{1}{3}, 4, 5, 6m, \frac{5}{7}, 1$$

Let's dive into numbers!

One: The 1 Chord and Its Dominance

What is the 1 chord?

The 1 chord is the most important chord to know how to hear. It's foundational and fundamental. It's *the* chord to which we will reference most of the others. It's like the President of the United States. Sure, the Vice President is important but less so than the President.

A 1–note that the word *chord* is not necessary–is built on the triad of the 1+3+5 notes of the major scale. Each of the three notes of the 1+3+5 are evenly spaced apart note to note. There are two full musical steps from the 1 note to the 3. There are two full steps between the 3 and the 5. For reference, this means there is a single white key between the 1 and the 3 and one white key between the 3 and the 5. If you are familiar with the piano, see the C Major chord diagramed below.

C MAJOR CHORD
-1 Chord-

Each note being evenly spaced apart means that the sound is solid and pleasant to our ears. We call these major chords. We'll discuss other types as well–like minor and diminished chords–but major chords are our main building blocks. They provide stability and are used often.

In the key of C, the 1 chord is C and is built using the notes C+E+G. You can rearrange those letters however you would like (called inversions) and you will still have a C chord.

How to hear and listen for the 1 chord.

To find a 1, listen for the chord that feels the most settled. When a song arrives on a 1, it's as if it has landed. However brief you may be on the 1 chord, it still feels home. It always helps to find the 1 chord in your song before you work to determine any of the others. You should be able to hear a 1 chord and know what it is. Let's use the key of C throughout the rest of this training. Play a C and let it be our foundation.

Play a C chord then move to an F chord then G and then land back on a C chord. Upon finishing at the C, you'll hear the progression settle. It's as if it left the station, went to two different stops along the way, and then returned home. That landing or settling back into C is how to hear the 1 chord. Again, it's the one that always feels most settled and secure in a progression. It's peaceful.

C MAJOR CHORD
-1 Chord-

F MAJOR CHORD
-4 Chord-

G MAJOR CHORD
-5 Chord-

C MAJOR CHORD
-1 Chord-

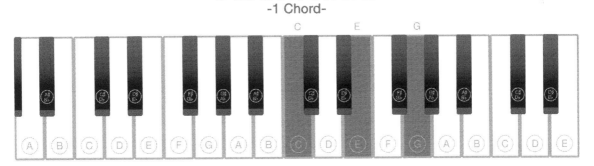

How popular is the 1 chord and what is the likelihood of hearing it in a song?

Most songs you'll listen to have at least a single 1 chord. In fact, it's often the first chord in a song. However, that is not always the case, so use our test to hear most of the song to listen for the settling nature of the 1 chord. When first listening to your song, try to listen for the 1 first. It will set you up to be able to hear all the others.

Practice hearing the 1 chord in these famous songs:

Artist: One Direction
Song: *What Makes You Beautiful*
Where is the 1 chord: First chord of the choruses

Artist: The Beatles
Song: *Let It Be*
Where is the 1 chord: First chord of the verses

Artist: Aretha Franklin
Song: *Respect*
Where is the 1 chord: First chord of the verses

Artist: Taylor Swift
Song: *Love Story*
Where is the 1 chord: First chord of the verses and choruses

Two: The 4 and 5: The Other Pillars

The 4 and 5 chords are pillars too

Building upon the 1 chord we spoke about above, the 4 and 5 chords relate most solidly to the 1. Let's use the key of C as an example throughout the rest of this section. It will help if you play these chords while you read along to hear the differences mentioned. In the key of C, the 1 chord is C. You guessed it! The 4 chord is an F chord and the 5 is G. These three numbers are the three pillar chords in any key. They are like the structural triangle that all the others derive. While the 1 chord is dominant, the 4 and 5 are also dominant and important chords in any key.

What is the 4 chord?

The 4 chord shares the root note of the 1 chord (which is the note C in our examples). What it doesn't share is the 4 and 6 notes, which is what makes it sound far different and easily recognizable. The notes are 4+6+1. The notes for the F chord are F+A+C.

F MAJOR CHORD
-4 Chord-

How to hear and listen for the 4 chord

The 4 chord is also known as the perfect fourth. It always sounds like it wants to resolve or fall back to a 1 chord. The only note that it shares with the 1 is the tonic note (or the root note of the scale), yet to the ear, it always sounds suspended or incomplete. If you are familiar with traditional hymns, the "Amen" at the end of "The Doxology" is a 4 chord that resolves to a 1. The 4 chord in the key of C is the F. Play an F and then let it resolve back to the 1, or C. You should notice a sort of settling sound as the chords resolve.

F MAJOR CHORD
-4 Chord-

C MAJOR CHORD
-1 Chord-

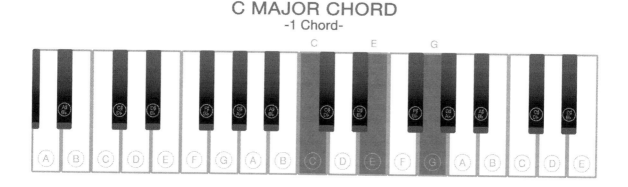

The 5 Chord

The 5 chord shares one important note with the 1 chord, much like the 4 chord did with the tonic note, but this time it is the 5 note. This makes the 5 chord have an opposing sound to the 1. Whereas the 4 chord sounds more complementary. A 5 chord is built as 5+7+2. 5 is the root note of this chord. In the key of C, it's the G chord and these notes would be G+B+D. Again, rearrange those notes however you would like and you still have a G chord.

G MAJOR CHORD
-5 Chord-

How to hear and listen for the 5 chord

In music theory, the 5 chord is called the dominant fifth. It's a springboard back to the 1. Play a G chord then move to the C. You will hear the dominant nature of the G and then the relief of landing on the C. What you're hearing is the 5 moving to a 1.

G MAJOR CHORD
-5 Chord-

C MAJOR CHORD
-1 Chord-

Now try the reverse. Play a C to a G. You'll hear the same two dominant chords interacting. The 1 to 5 has become a stair step or lifting sound. If you were to end a song on a 5, it would almost certainly feel unresolved.

C MAJOR CHORD
-1 Chord-

G MAJOR CHORD
-5 Chord-

A 5 also transitions smoothly to a 4 chord. Play a G (the 5) to an F (the 4) to the C (1 chord). This progression has a very distinct sound. It is as if the 5 chord wanted to get to a 4 chord and then the 4 wants to fall to a 1. The 5 causes musical unrest while the 4 and 1 chords are more settling.

G MAJOR CHORD
-5 Chord-

F MAJOR CHORD
-4 Chord-

C MAJOR CHORD
-1 Chord-

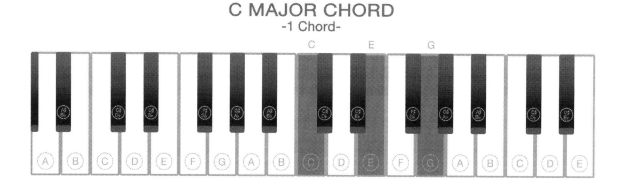

How popular are the 4 and 5 chords and what is the likelihood of hearing them in a song?

Much like the 1 chord, you'll likely hear a 4 and a 5 in most songs you'll listen to. You may hear the 5 slightly more than the 4. Be listening for both. See if you can distinguish the two. It doesn't matter which key you are playing in. I bet you'll be able to determine which chord is the 4 and which the 5.

Practice hearing the 4 chord in these famous songs:

Artist: Carly Rae Jepsen
Song: *Call Me Maybe*
Where is the 4 chord: First chord of the verses

Artist: Matchbox Twenty
Song: *Bed Of Lies*
Where is the 4 chord: First chord of the choruses

Practice hearing the 5 chord in these famous songs:

Artist: Journey
Song: *Don't Stop Believin'*
Where is the 4 chord: The second chord of the chord progression used in the intro, verses, and basically the rest of the song.

Artist: The Beatles
Song: *Hey Jude*
Where is the 4 chord: The second chord of the verses

Three: The 6m: Just A Dark 1 Chord

What is the 6m chord?

A 6m chord is simply a 1 chord with the bass note shifted down two notes. It's strong like a 1 chord and as easy to hear. It's our first minor chord. Use the lowercase *m* to denote minor for all minor chords. They tend to have a darker, sadder sound than their major chord counterparts. The 6m is used in about every pop song. You'll find it as often as the 1, 4, and 5 chords. Play a 1 chord, C, to our new 6m, Am, then to 5, G, then to 4, F. You'll hear this progression in thousands of songs.

C MAJOR CHORD
-1 Chord-

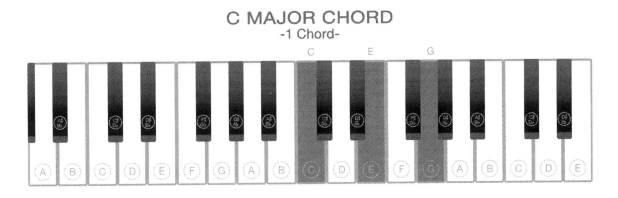

A MINOR CHORD
-6m Chord-

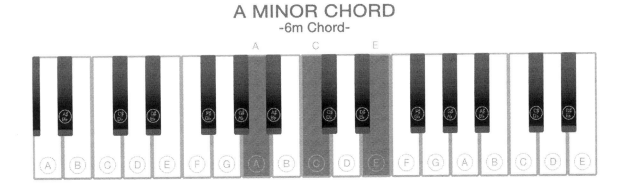

G MAJOR CHORD
-5 Chord-

F MAJOR CHORD
-4 Chord-

As noted above, the 6m and the 1 chord are built almost the same. In fact, a 6m^7 is made of the same notes as a 1, but the bass note is shifted downward by two steps. The notes from the 1 chord–or C in this case–are C+E+G. The notes in the 6m–or Am–are A+C+E. The only difference is a traded out G note in the C for an A note in the Am. That's why they sound so similar.

How to hear and listen for the 6m chord.

Since minor chords have a darker sound than brighter major chords they can be easier to hear. The 6m may be the darkest of all the minors. Most pop songs utilize at least one 6m. When you hear the chord change from a peppier tone, which is likely a 1, 4, or 5 chord, to a darker sound you can almost be assured it's a 6m. We will learn several other minors in the next few chapters, but the 6m is the most prominent.

How popular is the 6m chord and what is the likelihood of hearing it in a song?

The likelihood of hearing a 6m is extremely high in most songs. In fact, the only time you may not hear one is in children's music since it's a darker sound than the happier 1, 4, or 5 chords. Listen for the moment the chord moves to that darker, sadder tone.

Practice hearing the 6m chord in these famous songs:

Artist: The Beatles
Song: Let It Be
Where is the 6m chord: First chord of the choruses

Artist: Toto
Song: *Africa*
Where is the 6m chord: First chord of the choruses

Artist: Oasis
Song: *Wonderwall*
Where is the 6m chord: First chord of the intro and verses

Artist: Chris Tomlin
Song: *Our God*
Where is the 6m chord: First chord of the verses and the choruses

Four: The 2m: The New 5

What is the 2m chord?

The 2m chord is mostly a 4 chord with the bass note shifted down by two steps. Technically, the $2m^7$ is the 4 chord shifted, but the purpose is the same. A 2m chord is built as the 2+4+6 notes in the scale. Remember, a 4 chord is a 4+6+1. The difference between the 2m and the 4 being the 1 and 2 notes. Everything else is the same. The 2m in the key of C is Dm. The notes are D+F+A.

D MINOR CHORD
-2m Chord-

Typically, the 2m has either come from a 1 and feels like it has lifted the progression upward or it has fallen from a 4 chord. Try playing a 1 to 2m to 4.

C MAJOR CHORD
-1 Chord-

D MINOR CHORD
-2m Chord-

F MAJOR CHORD
-4 Chord-

Now try playing a 1 to 4 to 2m.

C MAJOR CHORD
-1 Chord-

F MAJOR CHORD
-4 Chord-

D MINOR CHORD
-2m Chord-

How to hear and listen for the 2m chord

A 2m is a minor chord, but I find it to be a little brighter or happier than the 6m we looked at in the last chapter. Some have said that the 2m is the new 5. What that means is that some songwriters have abandoned using the 5 chord in lieu of a 2m.

Distinguishing between a 2m and a 6m can be difficult at first. I find the 6m to be dark, while the 2m sounds lighter and softer.

How popular is the 2m chord and what is the likelihood of hearing it in a song?

The 2m is not as popular as the 1, 4, 5, and 6m. You will hear a 6m far more than a 2m. When you hear a minor sound you can assume a 6m until you play it and know it isn't correct. It would likely then be the 2m.

Practice hearing the 2m chord in these famous songs:

Artist: Aerosmith
Song: *I Don't Want To Miss A Thing*
Where is the 2m chord: Third chord of the chorus

Artist: Oasis
Song: *Little By Little*
Where is the 2m chord: Third chord of the chorus

Five: The "Over" or Passing Chords: ⅓, ⁵⁄₇, and ⁴⁄₁

What are the "over" or passing chords?

"Over" chords, or chords that look like fractions with one number on top of the other, are typically chords like the 1, 4, and 5, but with a shifted up bass note. For instance, a $^C/_E$ (which is a ⅓ in the key of C) would build as a normal C chord with the right hand on the piano, but the left hand would play an E note rather than the traditional C bass note. This brings a new sound to the strength of the chord. We use the term *over* because we pronounce them as "one over three" or "five over seven".

These are also called *passing chords*. It's because you will often play these types of chords while on the way to the next one while not hanging on them long. Sometimes they may simply be used for one or two beats and will not span an entire measure. They help you transition from one chord to the next.

Using a $^5/_7$ works best to get from a 1 to a 6m by walking down the scale: 1 to the $^5/_7$ to the 6m. Using the key of C, those chords are C to $^G/_B$ to Am.

C MAJOR CHORD
-1 Chord-

G/B MAJOR CHORD
-5/7 Chord-

A MINOR CHORD
-6m Chord-

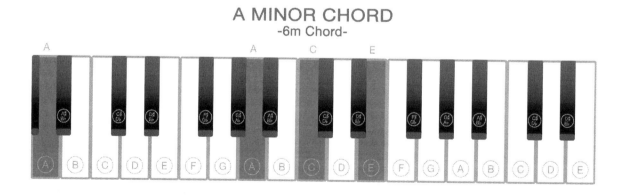

Now go up the scale by using a 1 to a ⅓ to a 4 or C to $^C/_E$ to F. We'll look at several popular passing chords below.

C MAJOR CHORD
-1 Chord-

C/E MAJOR CHORD
-1/3 Chord-

F MAJOR CHORD
-4 Chord-

The ⅓ Chord

Traditional music theory says that the chord scale plays 1 to 2m to 3m to 4. Instead of the 3m in popular music, we play a ⅓. This is simpler and sounds smoother. A ⅓ is just as it sounds: a full 1 chord with this bass note shifted up to a 3 note. The 1 chord is a 1+3+5 and then the shifted bass note is a 3. In the key of C, this chord is a C/E. The ⅓ has a sense of motion and movement to it and you'll typically only play it for a beat or two on your way to another more stable chord. Whereas, with a 1, 4, or 5 chord you may rest a full measure or even most of a verse or chorus on one of those. It has a sense of transition or motion to it.

The ⅝ Chord

Extremely similar to the ⅓, the ⅝ chord is simply a 5 chord with a shifted up 7 note in the bass. As another transition chord, these notes are 5+7+2 with the bass note being a 7. In the key of C, this is a G/B chord and is built G+B+D with the bass note being B. This chord is used often to transition from the 1 chord (C) to the 6m (Am).

The 4/1 Chord

While not a typical passing chord, the 4/1 is a standard "over" chord. It works and sounds much like a sus chord (we discuss chord suffices–like *sus*–in chapter 9). It's built with a complete 4 chord over top of a 1 as the bass note. The 4/1 has a suspended in air feel to it. It wants to resolve back to the 1 chord. You'll be able to hear it by playing a 4/1 (F/C in our key of C example) to a 1 (C).

F/C MAJOR CHORD
-4/1 Chord-

C MAJOR CHORD
-1 Chord-

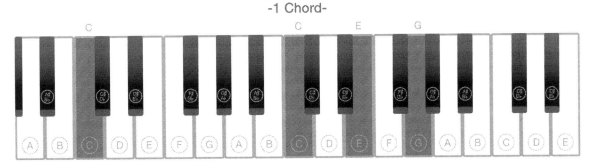

How to hear and listen for the ⅓, ⁵⁄₇, and ⁴⁄₁ chords

Remember, the ⅓ and ⁵⁄₇ chords are each standard 1 and 5 chords, but with shifted bass notes. If you are beginning to hear the 1 and 5 chords, then the shifted bass note will not lead you astray. The ⅓ and ⁵⁄₇ each have a passing chord sense to them. What this means is that they are not chords you play very long. Rather, you will use these to move to a more stable chord, like a 1, 4, or 5. They help to transition between chords well. You will notice a sense of upward or downward movement making them easier to hear.

The ⁴⁄₁ sounds mostly unstable but it is a chord that you can rest upon for a measure. It can last longer than the other "over" chords we have discussed. To hear the ⁴⁄₁ listen for a chord that sounds suspended on the root note of the key. It will likely resolve back to the 1 chord. When you hear that resolution, you've likely found a ⁴⁄₁ to 1.

How popular are the "over" and passing chords and what is the likelihood of hearing them in a song?

Over and passing chords are extremely popular. You'll likely hear them either overtly or subtly in every song you hear. Listen for quick moves from one dominant chord to the next, but it sounds like there is a chord passing between the two. That's your passing chord doing its work.

Six: The 3m and 7dim

What is the 3m chord?

Traditional music theory would say that the 3m and 7dim (pronounced *seven diminished*) are the final chords you should learn when learning major chord scales. Practically though, you will rarely play a 3m or 7dim. Especially in popular music. Instead, I recommend learning the ⅓ and ⁵⁄₇ chords. These are dominant chords with upward shifted bass notes, by the amount of two steps, from both the 1 and the 5 chords.

The 3m, much like we've seen with the other minor chords we've looked at, is a 5 chord with a shifted down bass note of two steps. This chord has a dark feeling when played in pop music. It is used, but rarely. The notes are 3+5+7. For the key of C, the chord is an Em and the notes are E+G+B. To hear this chord as it's used from time to time, play a 1 to 3m to 4.

C MAJOR CHORD
-1 Chord-

E MINOR CHORD
-3m Chord-

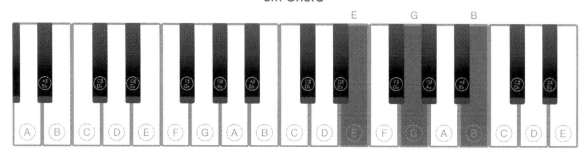

F MAJOR CHORD
-4 Chord-

What is the 7dim chord?

The 7dim (or diminished or the degrees symbol: °) is rarely used in pop music today. While this was not so even twenty or thirty years ago, the $5\!/\!7$ chord has taken its place in most cases. Diminished chords are utterly dark and normally fast passing chords. This means they are used to transition between main chords and are not held long. The notes are 7+2+4. You will notice that the 4 note in this chord is particularly drab. In the key of C, these notes are B+D+F. In the key of C, this chord is Bdim. To hear this chord used as it may be in the wild, play a 6m to 7dim to 1.

A MINOR CHORD
-6m Chord-

B DIMINISHED CHORD
-7dim Chord-

How to hear and listen for the 3m chord

The 3m chord has very particular properties. While not truly a passing chord, it would not be a chord with which to finish a song. The 3m is very dark in tone. In our example above of 1 to 3m to 4, you hear that the middle chord, being the 3m, feels like it temporarily leaves the key of C. It does not technically do so, but it does oddly catch the ear. The 3m sounds extremely dark and harsh to our ears. It provides richness to a chord progression because of its unusual nature.

How to hear and listen for the 7dim chord

The 7dim is hard to hear. It's not used often enough in popular music to give a perfect instance when you may hear it. Were it to be used, listen for an incredibly dissonant chord that is either coming to or from the 1 chord. Like the 3m–but even more so–the 7dim is extremely dark and drab sounding. It's not a chord that most songwriters will hang on long or even use.

How popular are the 3m and 7dim chords and what is the likelihood of hearing them in a song?

It's more likely that you will hear a 3m as compared to the 7dim. Neither are extremely popular choices. Of all the chords we've covered so far these two are the least likely to appear. When deciding what a chord may be in a song, do not begin with these two. Consider them only after you've exhausted that the unidentified chord isn't a 6m or 2m first.

Seven: The ♭7, 2, and 3: The Accidentals

What is the ♭7 chord?

Music has rules and some that are meant to be broken. It would be a terrible dictator. The ♭7 chord (pronounced *flat seven*) is used quite a bit, but one of the notes lies outside the major scale. The ♭7 chord employs the ♭7 note in the major scale as its foundation. Typically, the major seventh note in the scale is used, however, in certain cases, the ♭7 is used. The ♭7 chord is built as ♭7+2+4. Notice the 2 and 4. These notes give the chord stability in the key you are in. The ♭7 note is the outlier. In the key of C, the B♭ chord is the ♭7. Those notes are B♭+D+F. If you play the chords C, then B♭, F, and then back to C, you will hear the unique sound of the ♭7. It sounds both right and wrong at the same time. Music is awesome!

C MAJOR CHORD
-1 Chord-

B♭ MAJOR CHORD
-♭7 Chord-

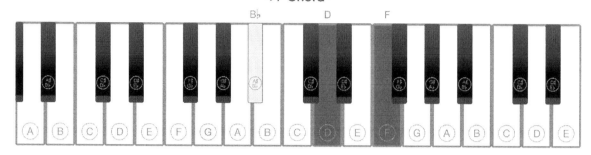

F MAJOR CHORD
-4 Chord-

C MAJOR CHORD
-1 Chord-

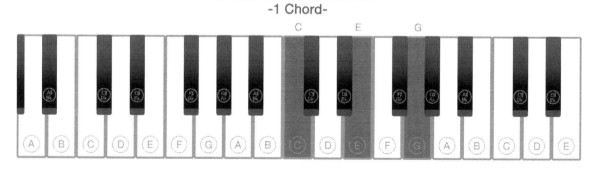

What is the 2 or 2-Major chord?

Similar to the ♭7 chord, the 2-Major chord, written as just a 2, has one note that does not belong in the laws of the major scale yet still works to our ears. The 2, or 2-Major chord, is built on–you guessed it–the 2 chord being major, rather than minor. I've used the term major after the number two only for the purpose distinguishing it from the 2m which would naturally occur in a key. As written you would not see the word major after the number 2. The 2-Major assumes these notes: 2+#4+6. Remember, the 2m was a 2+4+6. That #4 note brings a new identifiable character to a song. In the key of C, the 2-Major chord is D. Those notes are D+F#+A. This chord may be an integral part of a song when it is used, but most of the time it is to catch the surprise of the listener. I feel like I have heard it mostly at the end of bridges but before a final chorus. Perhaps it makes the song more interesting. It's also used heavily as the unique sounding chord in hymns.

C MAJOR CHORD
-1 Chord-

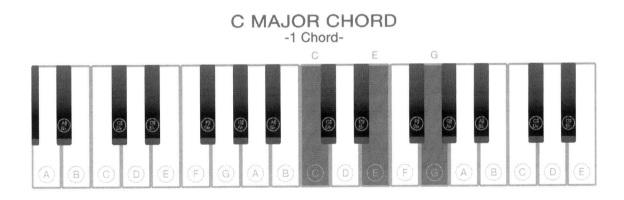

D MAJOR CHORD
-2 Chord-

F MAJOR CHORD
-4 Chord-

C MAJOR CHORD
-1 Chord-

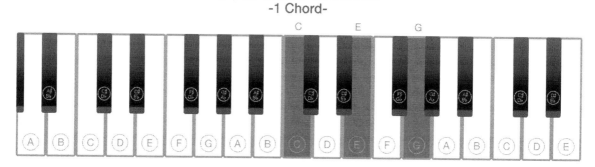

What is the 3-Major chord?

The 3-Major chord, or simply written as a 3, is another unique sounding outlier chord. To our ears it sounds a bit like the 2-Major, but with one important distinction. Rather than raising the fourth note of the scale up half a step like we did with the 2-Major, we lift the fifth note up a half step to create the unique sound of the 3. The 3-Major almost always precedes a 6m. Whereas the 2-Major doesn't have a typical use case because it works coming and going from many other dominant chords. If you hear an outlier chord and then immediately a 6m afterward it's likely the 3-Major. You'll hear how that sounds through the progression 1, 3, 6m, 1 below. You'll notice how the 3 sounds like it is lifting the progression up to the 6m.

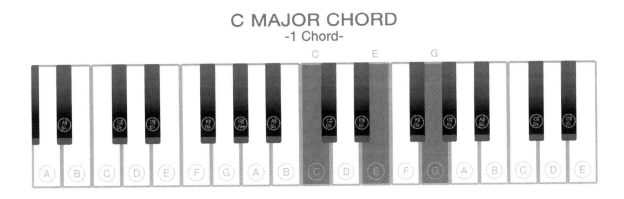

C MAJOR CHORD
-1 Chord-

E MAJOR CHORD
-3 Chord-

A MINOR CHORD
-6m Chord-

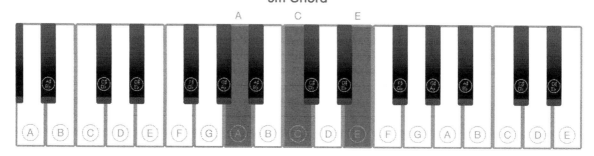

F MAJOR CHORD
-4 Chord-

How to hear and listen for the ♭7 chord

A ♭7 chord is as unique to the ear as a 1 chord. You cannot miss it. The ♭7 chord is an outlier and sounds like it. It feels like an automatic departure. The ear hears it almost as if it does not belong. The power in this chord is that it sounds so strange but still works. Many bridges of songs employ this chord to add an element of surprise and difference that makes the bridge stand out from the rest of the song.

How to hear and listen for the 2-Major chord

You will only hear this type of chord from time to time. The 2-Major has an outlier #4 note of the major scale in it. What that means is that the ear hears the odd grouping of 2+#4+6, rather than the typical 2+4+6 notes which is a minor chord and uses only the standard notes in the major scale. This #4 note surprises the ear. Listen for a lifting sound when you hear a chord that surprises the ear. It's never one that ends a section. Rather, it leads to a more dominant chord in the key. It's different from the ♭7 because it doesn't feel like a full departure from the key.

How to hear and listen for the 3-Major chord

The 3-Major is rare enough that you'll only hear it once in a blue moon in pop music. Listen for a strange-sounding chord that leads to a minor chord directly following it. It's likely the 3-Major. You may even hear a $^3/\#5$ ($^E/G\#$ in the key of C) with the 3-Major chord having the shifted up #5 bass note. This is nearly always followed by a 6m chord in a progression.

How popular are the ♭7, 2, and 3 chords, and what is the likelihood of hearing them in a song?

You are more likely to hear the ♭7 than a 2 or 3. And you're more likely to hear the 2 than you are the 3. Each of these chords is used more sparingly in songwriting, so when trying to determine a chord progression, begin with your more standard 1, 4, 5, and 6m chords and work your way toward these if those main chords aren't working. Try these when the chord sounds outside of the key or as an outlier sound.

Eight: The Most Common Chord Patterns (You'll Hear These Everywhere)

Overview

There are four important chord progressions that you'll hear in thousands upon thousands of pop and worship songs. If you listen for some of the "tells" for each you'll recognize them easily. The key is to determine the rise and fall of these progressions. As you practice listening for them you'll become proficient in finding them right away.

1, 5, 6m, 4

Likely the most common progression of all time, 1, 5, 6m, 4 can be found in tons of songs. It begins with the dominant 1 chord. This feels stable and a strong beginning point. Then, it moves to the equally dominant 5 chord. This feels like it's taken a step up and is on to a new landing. Then it moves to the darker 6m chord. This is the only minor chord in the progression so it's easy to determine. It's also a 6m, which is strong sounding like the 1 chord, and not the weaker sounding 2m chord. Last, the entire progression falls to the 4 chord. It has the sound of a long drop to the 4. While the 4 sounds beautiful, it wants to fall back to the 1 chord, which is where the progression began.

6m, 4, 1, 5

You'll hear the progression 6m, 4, 1, 5 often. It's the same progression as the first we looked at above, but with the 6m beginning the series rather than the 1. It makes the start of the progression sound darker than when it begins with the 1. The rise and fall of each chord sounds the same as our first progression.

4, 1, 6m, 5

The progression 4, 1, 6m, 5 is fun because our ears perceive two different falls. A 4 to 1 move has a sense of the 4 falling down to a 1. The 6m to 5 has a fall or step down from the 6m to a 5.

1, 2m, 4, 5

The 1, 2m, 4, 5 series has almost a progressive stair-step effect. Each change is only moving upward one sound at a time. The 1 moves up to the 2m. The 2m up to the 4–we did skip 3 because it's not one of our dominant chords. The last move is from the 4 to a 5.

Nine: Going A Little Beyond: Chord Suffices

Chord suffices: adding color to a chord

Perhaps a little beyond the scope of this book, once you know how to hear what the number a chord is, it's useful to hear how some of the main chords are modified. We call these modifications chord *suffices*–the plural of the word *suffix*. You've likely seen these types of chords written out before. For example, Am^7–spoken: *A minor seven*–is an Am chord with an additional seventh note in the Am scale added to the end of the built chord. Chord suffices add flair or *color* to a chord. Below, we will look at several of the main suffices you'll come across. There are even more beyond these, but this is a great starting point.

7

One of the most common suffices is the 7. You'll see C^7, D^7, E^7, and so on. A 7 suffix assumes that you add the $\flat$7 note of the major scale to a major chord. It may sound like a weird rule–especially when you look at the Maj7 chord that is next in this chapter–but a 7 assumes a note that is not in the major scale. The chord will play $1+3+5+\flat7$. So a C^7 is played $C+E+G+B\flat$. It's one of the easiest suffices for our ears to distinguish because it sounds twangy. It's used tremendously in country music and in traditional hymns. It's also often used as a modification to a 5 chord. For instance, if you play C, F, G^7, C, you'll hear how the 5, when using the 7 modifier, brings the progression back to 1 in a way that is pleasant. Another way that 7 modifiers are used is by adding a 7 to a 2Maj chord. Typically a 2 chord in a popular chord progression is minor: 1, 2m, 4, 1. However, building the 2 major by adding a 7 creates a new progression with a smooth sound. Play a C, D^7, F, C. That new progression of 1, 2^7, 4, 1 adds options to songs you may write. It's often used in pop and soul music and also traditional hymns.

C7 CHORD
-7 Chord Suffix-

Maj7

A Major 7 chord (written as Maj7, note the capital *M*) is a common chord. It's jazzy in its sound and is soft in its nature. The Maj7 chord is made by playing a standard 1+3+5 major chord and also adding the 7th note in the scale. You'll hear this chord often in Jazz music, slower pops songs, and contemporary worship music. You can hear how a Maj7 sounds by playing a CMaj7, which are these notes combined: C+E+G+B.

CMaj7 CHORD
-Maj7 Chord Suffix-

m⁷

A minor 7 chord (written as m^7, note the lower case *m*) is a minor chord with a minor 7 note modifier. While the Maj7 chord adds the major seventh note of the major scale, the m^7 utilizes the minor seventh of the minor scale. A major scale has no flattened notes, while the minor scale is made as 1, 2, ♭3, 4 5, ♭6, ♭7, 1. This means that our ears perceive this scale as darker or even sad in tone. The m^7 chord is a subtitle shift from its derivative, the m or minor chord. You'll hear the distinction in the softness of the chord heard than its more solid minor counterpart. Here's how to build a Cm^7 chord: C+E♭+G+B♭. Compare the sound of the Cm^7 to the darker Cm: C+E♭+G.

Cm7 CHORD
-m7 Chord Suffix-

2 and add9

A 2, or often seen as an add9, is a common chord suffix. The 2 adds the second note of the major scale to a major chord. For instance, a C^2 adds the D note to the already built C chord, meaning it now plays as C+D+E+G. 2 chords sound rich and delightful. They are typically used to tie a 1 chord to a 4 chord because the 2 note in the 4 chord keeps the same note–the 5 note in the 1 chord–the same. It brings continuity to the transition between the 1 and the 4. You will likely see a 2 written as an add9. All this means is that the 2 note is added at the top of the chord rather than at the bottom or in the middle. A Cadd9 means that the chord would be built C+E+G+D. It has the same richness of the 2 chord, but now the 2 note is further spaced out allowing the distinction to be more present to our ears. Try both on a piano and hear for yourself the richness of the 2 and add9 chords.

C2 CHORD
-2 Chord Suffix-

Cadd9 CHORD
-add9 Chord Suffix-

sus

A *sus* chord is one of the most pleasant of the suffices. The name *sus* is short for "suspended" and moves or suspends the 3 note in a major chord to the 4th. The new chord is built 1+4+5. A sus chord has a lifted or suspended in air sound and wants to resolve back to its original major chord. Play a Csus by using the notes C+F+G and let it resolve back to the C chord C+E+G. Going between the two you'll hear the suspended nature of the Csus resolving to the original sound of the C.

Csus CHORD
-sus Chord Suffix-

5

If you are a guitar player and have used *power chords* in the past, you've been playing 5 suffices and perhaps not known it. For those not guitarists, the 5 suffix means that a major chord has been stripped of its 3 note, leaving only the 1 and 5 notes. This makes for an extremely strong sounding chord, but since there is no 3 note, there is no major or minor chord distinction. The 3 note in a chord provides what is known as color. If the 3 note is in the major scale the entire chord becomes major. If the 3 note has been flattened it makes the entire chord minor. In a 5 chord suffix, there is no 3. Instead, the chord is clear and often used in musical accompaniment. Play a C chord using C+E+G, or 1+3+5, and then remove the E, or 3, to create the C^5 chord, which is now only C+G, or 1+5. Transition back and forth between the two to hear the distinction. You'll use chords with the 5 suffix anytime you want to chord to sound lighter and add the 3 note back in when you want the chord more defined and heavier sounding. Experiment with these. You'll find what your ear prefers and when to use each.

C5 CHORD
-5 Chord Suffix-

6

The 6 suffix is a tougher chord to recognize. It's a typical major chord, but the 5 note has been replaced by a 6 so it's built 1+3+6. The sound is a bit like the sound made by a train's horn. It's strong and heavy. Hear the difference between the C chord, played C+E+G, and the C^6, played C+E+A. You'll hear the defined sound of the C while the C^6 sounds flabbier or less defined. Chords with a 6 chord suffix are used most often when moving from a 1 to a 5 chord where the 5 has a 6 as its suffix. Try playing C (C+E+G) to G^6 (G+B+E). You'll hear the distinction.

C6 CHORD
-6 Chord Suffix-

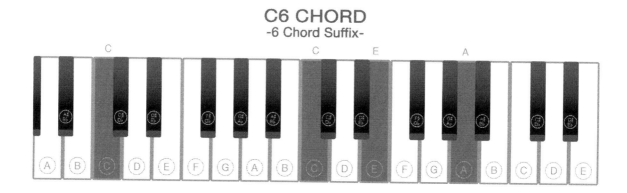

Final Greetings and Pop Quiz

You've made it!

You should now be able to easily recognize the 1, 4, and 5 chords when you listen to your favorite songs! You'll continue to get better and better with practice. You've got the basic and future building blocks for becoming extremely successful!

You can hear songs in numbers, not just chords in a key. You're able to stand on stage, for the most part, without any notes, charts, or sheet music. This all comes with the familiarity of knowing what each chord and number sounds like. The 1 chord is distinctly different from a 4 or a 5. A 6m and a 2m sound different from one another, even though they are both minor chords. It takes a fair amount of practice, but at some point, it becomes second nature.

Pop quiz for some numbers

Let's take a pop quiz using some famous songs and see if you can recognize the chord progressions using numbers for each. Here's how this will work. Look at the name of the song and artist and listen to the chorus a few times through YouTube or your music player. Write down what the number sequence is and then compare it to the answers below. Hopefully, you'll not only be able to correctly hear the patterns but also see how many famous songs share the same number patterns. Here we go!

Song: *Don't Stop Believin'*
Artist: Journey

Chorus Pattern: 1 + 5 + 6m + 4

Song: *Can You Feel The Love Tonight?*
Artist: Elton John

Chorus Pattern: 1 + 5 + 6m + 4

Song: *Octopus's Garden*
Artist: The Beatles

Chorus Pattern: 1 + 6m + 4 + 5

Song: *I Will Always Love You*
Artist: Whitney Houston and also Dolly Parton's version

Chorus Pattern: 1 + 6m + 4 + 5

Song: *Africa*
Artist: Toto

Chorus Pattern: 6m + 4 + 1 + 5

Recommended Resources

Piano Chords One and Two

I cannot highly recommend enough my *Piano Authority Series* of books: *Piano Chords One* and *Two*. Quickly translate everything that you know about chords to the piano. Written much like a manual, you'll learn the most important chords to play on the piano and how to play the many versions of them. If you've ever longed to be able to play through songs on the piano and accompany yourself, these two books will help you do that. Grab a copy of each and see what you can accomplish!

Worship Guitar In Six Weeks

Worship Guitar In Six Weeks is a perfect primer for anyone interested in joining a worship team as a rhythm guitar player. The premise is that you need only a few quick tools to learn before you have enough knowledge and skill to play with a group. It teaches the parts that make up the guitar, a few important chords, how to strum, and a bit more. I recommend this book for the beginner. The pacing is perfect!

42 Guitar Chords Everyone Should Know

Using *42 Guitar Chords Everyone Should Know*, you'll take a deeper dive into how guitar chords relate one to another. You'll learn how to move quickly between G to D to Em to Cadd9–each chord important for the key of G. *42 Chords* is a great next step after *Worship Guitar In Six Weeks*.

Fast Guitar Chord Transitions

One of the neatest books I've ever worked on is *Fast Guitar Chord Transitions*. Most guitar manuals will show you how to play chords. This includes finger placement, which strings to strum, and so on. But, one overlooked aspect of the guitar is that transitioning between chords is as important as knowing the chords themselves. In *Fast Guitar Chord Transitions*, I walk a guitarist through the steps of transitioning all of the most popular chord moves you'll need to know. The book is arranged based on the key of a song in which you may be playing. It's worth every penny!

Guitar Secrets Revealed

Guitar Secrets Revealed is a book for the intermediate player looking for professional-level insights. Use this manual to get inside the mind of the pro. Find out how they think. You'll learn practicable, actionable music theory that you can implement today. Plus, find out how to use more unique guitar chord shapes that work like inversions of basic chords. All in all, this book takes a guitar player to the next level–maybe even up two levels!

Appendix: Numbers for Each Key

Chord Diagram

Each key has a unique chord scale progression. Use the diagram below as a reference as you continue to grow hearing chords as numbers. It doesn't matter which key you are in, the numbers are the same. It's only the chord names that change relative to the key.

Chord Families

Key	1	2m	1/3	4	5	6m	5/7	1
G	G	Am	G/B	C	D	Em	D/F#	G
Ab	Ab	Bbm	Ab/C	Db	Eb	Fm	Eb/G	Ab
A	A	Bm	A/C#	D	E	F#m	E/G#	A
Bb	Bb	Cm	Bb/D	Eb	F	Gm	F/A	Bb
B	B	C#m	B/D#	E	F#	G#m	F#/A#	B
C	C	Dm	C/E	F	G	Am	G/B	C
Db	Db	Ebm	Db/F	Gb	Ab	Bbm	Ab/C	Db
D	D	Em	D/F#	G	A	Bm	A/C#	D
Eb	Eb	Fm	Eb/G	Ab	Bb	Cm	Bb/D	Eb
E	E	F#m	E/G#	A	B	C#m	B/D#	E
F	F	Gm	F/A	Bb	C	Dm	C/E	F
Gb	Gb	Abm	Gb/Bb	Cb (B)	Db	Ebm	Db/F	Gb

About The Author

Why so many people learn music from Micah

The best instructors teach to the student, not to the curriculum. The curriculum serves as a vehicle for learning. It's a tool of sorts. One of the best parts of teaching music lessons–in this case, learning to hear numbers–is the ability to help a student learn at just the right pace. I've found that my job as an educator is to always be encouraging my students to take one step more than he or she may not have taken on their own. The only thing to sort out is at which pace you perform best.

I've been teaching piano, guitar, ukulele, and music theory courses for more than ten years. In fact, that's why I've written five books for guitar, two for piano, and one for ukulele to date. My emphasis has always been, and will likely always be, in commercial music. While I think classical music is worth studying, I always find myself improvising over the original melodies–even those of the greats, like Beethoven, Brahms, or Bach. It's human nature to explore or be curious and I love teaching with the mindset that the music greats of the past are like proven guides. They shouldn't always be copied, but rather those from whom to learn.

Living twenty-five miles from downtown Nashville, TN has provided me and my family privileges in music that I'm certain are not given in every town. You can't throw a stone in Nashville without hitting someone who is personally or has a family member in the music industry. Not one of us takes the Grand Ole Opry backstage tour because we all plan to be there as a music artist someday. Even if we sing and play music for Jesus as Christian or worship artists, we still likely won't spend the time or money for that tour. We plan to perform on that ageless circle that lands center-stage someday ourselves.

My wife of more than ten years is wonderful and my greatest joy. We have four kids who keep us very busy and quite exhausted! We also keep two Yorkshire Terrier dogs who I'm sure my wife would give away for less than the price of two movie tickets. I love them though. Plus, we just got an all-black labradoodle.

It's an honor to help you work toward your goals. Being able to hear chords may unlock creativity in you that has been buried deep within for years. It's time to let it out!

Blessings,

-Micah Brooks
www.micahbrooks.com
Find me on Facebook, Twitter, LinkedIn, Instagram, and Amazon.com

Connect With Micah Brooks

Signup for Micah Brooks emails to stay up to date

Subscribe to the Micah Brooks Company "Stay Connected" email list for the latest book releases. This email list is always free and intended to deliver high-value content to your inbox. Visit the link below to signup.

www.micahbrooks.com

Contact Micah

Email Micah Brooks at micahbrooks.com/contact. I want to know who you are. It's my privilege to respond to your emails personally. Please feel free to connect.

Please share this book with your friends

If you would like to share your thanks for this book, the best thing you can do is to tell a friend about *Piano Chords Three: Numbers* or buy them a copy. You can also show your appreciation for this book by leaving a five-star review on Amazon:

www.amazon.com

Follow Micah Brooks:

Facebook: @micahbrooksofficial
Twitter: @micahbrooksco
LinkedIn: Micah Brooks
Instagram: @micahbrooksco
Amazon: amazon.com/author/micahbrooks

If you have trouble connecting to any of these social media accounts, please visit www.micahbrooks.com.

Sing to him a new song;
play skillfully, and shout for joy.

Psalm 33:3 (NIV)

Made in the USA
Columbia, SC
24 January 2025

52402211R00039